MW00891167

KNOWLEDGE ENCYCLOPEDIA

HUMAN BODY
STOMACH & DIGESTIVE SYSTEM

(An imprint of Prakash Books Pvt. Ltd.)

Wonder House Books
Corporate & Editorial Office
113-A, 1st Floor, Ansari Road,
Daryaganj, New Delhi-110002
Tel +91 11 2324 7062-65

Printed in 2020 in India

ISBN : 9789389931228

Table of Contents

WE ARE WHAT WE EAT

We are the atoms and molecules of the food that we eat. We need to spend a lot of energy and time getting food from the environment. We have a dedicated organ system in our body to turn this food into something our body can use. Our **digestive system** evolved to convert the food we eat into energy. The other organ systems like the circulatory system, nervous system and respiratory system, exist to support the digestive system.

The digestive system is a complex system, beginning with teeth, which break down food in smaller bits, the stomach, which dissolves these pieces into a semi-solid mass, the intestine, which breaks them down into molecules and absorbs them into our body, and the anus, which removes the undigested bits.

Scientists who study the evolution of animals suggest that our body plan is really a tube-within-a-tube. They even suggest that this body plan is the same in all organisms, from the tiniest worms to the biggest whales. The inner tube is our digestive system, from mouth to anus, while the outer tube is our body enclosed by the skin, with our arms sticking out. Between these is the space in which all our organs function.

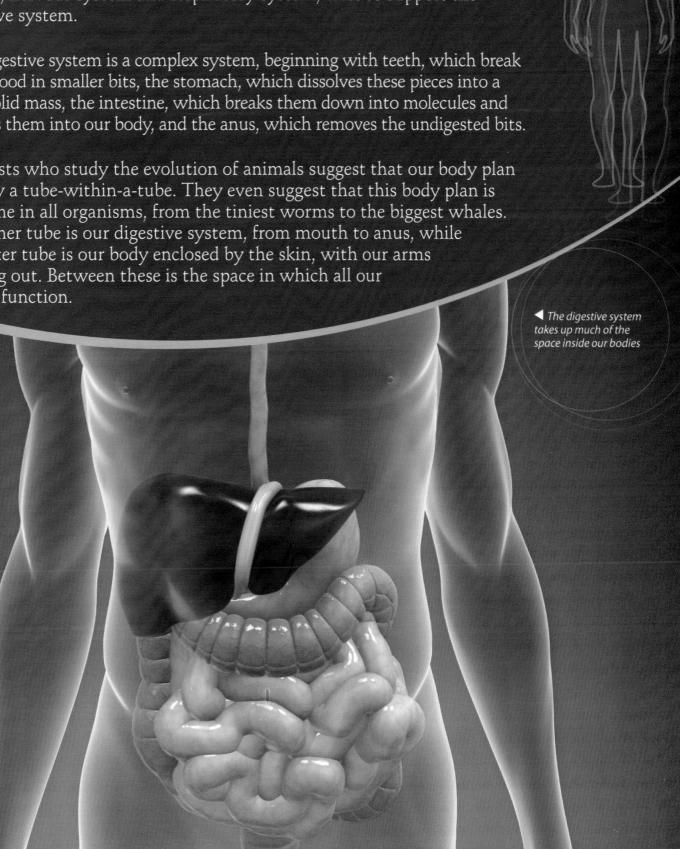

◄ *The digestive system takes up much of the space inside our bodies*

The First Bite

As you take the first bite of your meal, several parts of your body get to work. The first of these are your jaws, teeth and tongue. You use them to chew the food you eat into smaller bits. This makes it easier to digest the food. If you do not chew your food, some of it might remain undigested, so your stomach and intestines would have to work harder. So, do not eat too quickly or just swallow your food, but take the time to chew.

▲ *During winter, cracks might appear on the lips. Use a lip balm to heal your lips*

The Lips

The lips close the mouth and prevent food from falling out. Our lips allow us to talk properly. If you eat spicy food, you might feel a burning sensation on your lips. Similarly, while drinking a hot beverage, you might feel the warmth on your lips. This happens because your lips have nerve endings so that you can feel the food you are eating. The skin on your lips is very thin, so it can become dry and cracked in winter. During this season, it is a good idea to use a balm to provide moisture to the lips.

▶ *Our jaws have the strongest muscles in our body*

The Jaws

Though we bite and chew with our teeth, they cannot move by themselves. We move our jaws to make the teeth move. By opening and closing the mouth, we help our teeth bite, crush and grind the food. The upper jaw is called the **maxilla**, while the lower is called the **mandible**. The jaw muscles are very powerful. The mandible closes with a force of 112 kg.

💡 Isn't It Amazing!

The Australian Saltwater Crocodile has the world's strongest jaws, with a force of about 16,458 Newtons or 1678 kg. (Newtons is a unit of force.) But, the jaw muscles of this crocodile are so weak, that you can hold them shut with a rubber band!

▲ *Crocodiles can quickly snap their jaws shut with the powerful closing muscles of their jaws. However, their jaws are too weak to open them as quickly*

The Tongue

Our tongue presses food against the roof of the mouth, crushing it. It senses how hot or cold food is. We taste the food that we eat because it has thousands of tiny cells called taste buds. We have different kinds of taste buds to check the taste of sweet, salty, sour and bitter food.

The tongue is the most flexible organ of our body, made up of several tiny muscles. When the vocal cords in the throat (larynx) make sounds, the tongue's movement along the floor of the mouth, the roof and the teeth, turn them into the sounds we recognise, like A, B, C, D and so on, arranged into words. The tongue muscles are controlled by special areas of the brain that enable them to move correctly so that we say the words right.

 ▶ *Different taste buds on different parts of the tongue help taste distinct flavours*

Sweet   Sour   Salty   Bitter

Drool

Drool, or saliva, which is the scientifically correct term, helps us chew our food. It is made in salivary glands, which are found below the tongue and behind the throat. If your mouth did not have saliva, you would get a very dry mouth, making it difficult to chew and swallow food.

▶ *Babies cannot control their drooling. As adults, we might drool while we are sleeping*

The Throat

The throat is at the front of the neck. It has the thyroid gland, the food pipe, the wind pipe and the voice box. The back of the neck has the spinal cord. The **thyroid gland** makes the **thyroid hormone**, which tells your body to make energy from the food you eat. The food pipe carries food from the mouth to the stomach, while the wind pipe carries air from your nose to the lungs. They cross each other at the **pharynx**. The pharynx has a little lid-like organ called the epiglottis, which closes the windpipe when the food you just swallowed is being sent to the stomach.

⊛ Incredible Individuals

Some conjurers perform a special trick of swallowing a whole sword! They can do this because they can overcome their **gag reflex**. This is your body's way to stop choking when something touches the back of your mouth.

Teeth & Gums

We need our teeth not only to bite and chew food, but also to be able to talk to people properly. From the time we are 1 year old, till about 12 years, we have 24 milk teeth. Once those fall out, we get a new set of 32 teeth which we keep throughout most of our lives. They begin to fall out when we become old, but not if we are healthy. The teeth join the tongue for another job—making many different kinds of sound, so that we can talk to our friends!

 ## Teeth

Our teeth are arranged in two rows, in the upper and lower jaws. They do many things for us.

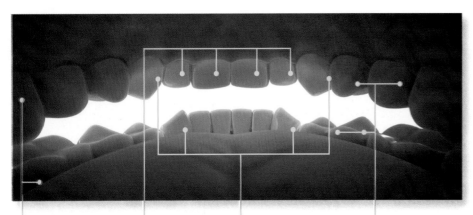

| The last three teeth on each side of both jaws (making twelve in all) are the molars, that grind food into a paste that can be swallowed. | The front eight teeth (four above, four below) are called incisors. They help bite off the food. | In each jaw, there is one tooth to the left of the incisors and one to the right. Together, they make up four teeth called canines. These tear off hard bits of food. | The next two on each side of both jaws (making eight in all) are premolars. |

▲ *The inside of our mouth, showing the tongue and teeth*

▶ *Healthy gums make for healthy teeth*

 ## Gums

The gums are the parts of the jaw which hold the teeth in place. Keeping your gums healthy by brushing everyday will make sure that your teeth do not fall out!

A 1.8 million-year-old skull found in Georgia (the country) by scientists in 2005, had only one tooth left. This showed that the person had lived to a very old age till they had lost their teeth and were eating with their gums.

 ## Gingivitis

Gingivitis is what doctors call a painful inflammation of the gums, which may cause bleeding and bad breath (halitosis). It is caused by bacteria which thrive in your gums if you do not brush them properly.

Parts of a Tooth

Each tooth is made of two parts—a root and a crown. The root is deep inside the gums and has nerves and blood vessels in it, which link to the jaw through the root canal. The crown of the tooth, made of calcium carbonate, does all the work. It has an inner part called dentin and an outer, harder part called enamel. It is important to take care of your crowns, by brushing them every day. Otherwise bacteria grow in the teeth and make holes called **cavities**, which can become very painful. If the cavity goes very deep, you need a **root canal operation** to fill it in.

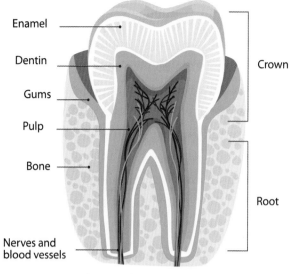

Enamel

Dentin

Gums

Pulp

Bone

Crown

Root

Nerves and blood vessels

▲ *Parts of a healthy tooth*

In Real Life

The last molars on each side of the jaw are called wisdom teeth. They do not come out until you are 20 years or older. For many people, sadly, there is not enough space in the jaw for the wisdom teeth to come out properly, so they cause a lot of pain. Then these teeth have to be removed by the dentist.

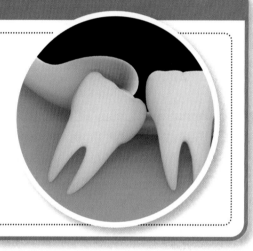

▶ *A wisdom tooth not growing properly*

Tooth Decay

When you do not brush your teeth regularly or properly, a powdery, yellow plaque forms over your teeth. This is made of tiny bits of food and the bacteria that grow on them. If you allow the plaque to remain, the bacteria in them invade the gaps between your teeth and then their crowns, forming **caries**. This is the start of dental cavities. Once they form, brushing will not remove them. You have to go to the dentist, who will have to drill your teeth to remove the decay and put in a cement filling or remove the tooth altogether.

Isn't It Amazing!

A shark's teeth never stop growing. When they fall out, they are replaced by new teeth. Through its life, a shark may grow and lose up to 35,000 teeth.

▶ *A shark showing a row of its upper teeth*

Hunger & Thirst

Did you know that your brain plays a role in digestion? The brain is the part of our body which finds out that we are running out of energy and water. Then it tells our stomach to start rumbling or our throat to feel dry—and we start to feel hungry or thirsty!

Our body makes many chemicals called **hormones**. They travel through the blood to various organs. Together with nerves, these hormones tell our body to start or stop eating, to transfer digested food into the blood so that it reaches all tissues and to turn them into energy.

▶ *We can have a variety of foods and beverages to quench our hunger and thirst*

Feeling Hungry

There is a small region in the brain called the hunger centre. When the stomach is empty, it makes a hormone called ghrelin. Ghrelin passes through the blood to the brain's hunger centre, which then makes you feel hungry. This feeling makes your body start wanting food.

During an infection, the body sometimes switches off the hunger centre, so that you do not eat and allow the infectious pathogen to get food.

Feeling Full

It is very important to have some fat in your diet. Fat not only provides a lot of energy, but also helps the body know when to stop eating. Once you have started eating food, the intestine starts digesting food into the molecules that make it up—fats, proteins, sugars, vitamins and minerals.

All these are taken into the blood, which gives it to the tissues. The tissue that takes up fat is called adipose tissue. When it has taken in enough fat, it makes a hormone called leptin. Leptin tells the brain's hunger centre to switch off and you start feeling full. The small intestine makes another hormone called incretin, which in turn tells the pancreas to make the hormone insulin. Insulin tells the brain that there is enough sugar in the blood.

If you eat too fast, your body does not have enough time to digest and know that you have eaten enough. You end up overeating! That is why we should eat slowly and chew our food. Some people have a medical condition in which they cannot switch off their hunger centres. They keep on eating and sometimes this leads to obesity.

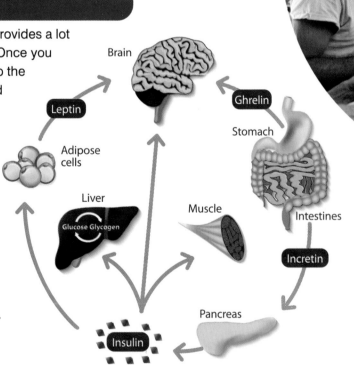

Brain

Ghrelin

Leptin

Stomach

Adipose cells

Liver

Glucose Glycogen

Muscle

Intestines

Incretin

Pancreas

Insulin

▲ *The diagram represents the process from hunger to satiation*

▲ *Your brain's thirst centre gets activated when your body is running low on water*

🧍 Feeling Thirsty

Alongside the hunger centre, the brain also has a thirst centre. When your body is running out of water, your blood becomes thicker and its pressure drops. This tells the brain that you need more water. It makes your throat feel dry, so you look for water. You open the fridge and cannot decide whether to have water, or gulp cola and hope nobody finds out!

Too much salt in your body also makes you feel thirsty. If you have not had enough water, the salt builds up in your body, and you start feeling dehydrated. This may make you dizzy. If you get dehydrated, take sips of water slowly, instead of drinking lots in one go.

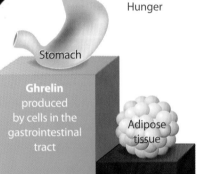

Ghrelin — Leptin
Hunger

Ghrelin — Leptin
Satiety

Stomach

Ghrelin produced by cells in the gastrointestinal tract

Adipose tissue

Leptin

Leptin hormone made by adipose cells

Ghrelin

Before eating

After eating

▲ *Ghrelin is a hormone that makes us feel hungry, while leptin makes us feel full*

▲ *We should avoid overeating as it could lead to many health problems*

👨‍⚕️ In Real Life

Doctors and nutritionists recommend that we have a heavy breakfast and a light dinner. Yet most of us do the exact opposite. Scientists have found that this is because of our circadian rhythm, the brain processes that govern our daily behaviour. It makes us eat well since the brain expects that we will not get food for the next several hours. It also reduces hunger so that we do not wake up and spoil our rest because we feel hungry.

▲ *Traditional English breakfast*

⭐ Incredible Individuals

A hunger strike is a form of protest in which people go hungry for days till their protest is heard. Mahatma Gandhi of India was famous for going on hunger strikes to protest against the atrocities of British colonial rule.

The Stomach

Think of digestion and you immediately think of the stomach.
It controls the pace of digestion and also makes a lot of
hormones that communicate with the different parts of the
body to either prepare to eat something, or to digest the
eaten food and turn it into energy.

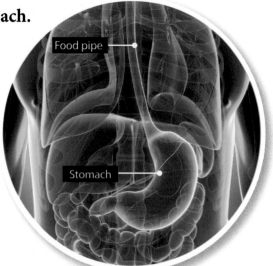

Getting Food to the Stomach

Between the throat and the stomach is a long pipe that passes
between the lungs—the oesophagus, also called the food pipe.
But food does not drop down it like water flows through a pipe.
The oesophagus has to make the food go down, by squeezing and
expanding (peristalsis). Between the oesophagus and stomach is a
muscle called the sphincter, which prevents the stomach's acid from
getting out.

▲ *The food pipe and the stomach*

Inside the Stomach

The stomach is a little like a balloon. It swells up as you
eat food. But unlike a balloon, it has very tough walls so
that it does not burst. The walls are made of three layers.
The outer wall is made of muscles, the middle layer has
arteries, veins and nerves, while the inner wall is made
of thousands of tiny folds called gastric pits.

The gastric pits make acid. This acid is released into
the stomach when you start eating, and it breaks up
the food into smaller chemical bits. The stomach also
makes an enzyme called pepsin, which breaks up the
proteins that you eat as part of your food into smaller
bits called peptides.

The stomach muscles contract and expand when the
stomach is full of food. This makes the stomach churn,
mixing up the food with the acid and pepsin. This helps
speed up digestion.

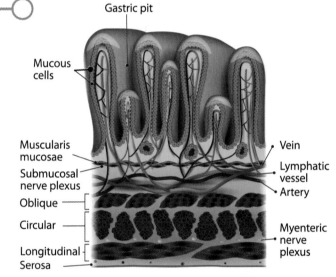

▲ *The stomach does more than just digest food. It also makes many hormones that control digestion and hunger*

💡 Isn't It Amazing!

If you have ever visited a farm, you
might have been told that a cow has
four stomachs. Actually, the stomach
of a cow is so large that it is divided
into four parts. This is because the
grass and leaves that cows eat are
hard to break down and therefore,
need a lot of time and space, in order
for them to be digested.

▶ *Cows have a stomach divided into four parts that help them digest grass and leaves better*

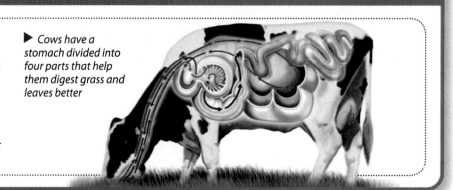

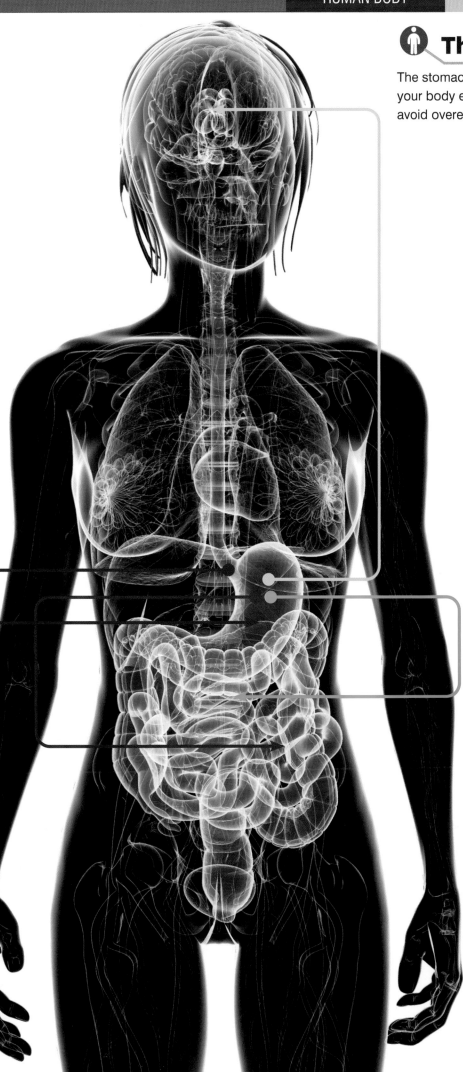

The Hormone Factory

The stomach makes a lot of hormones that help your body eat at the right time, eat enough and avoid overeating.

● When food enters the stomach, the stomach makes gastrin which tells the gastric pits to release pepsin. It also makes histamine which tells the gastric pits to release acid and serotonin, which tells the stomach muscle to start churning.

● Once you have eaten enough, somatostatin tells the stomach to stop and push the food into the small intestine. It also tells the pancreas and small intestine to stop performing their functions.

● When it is empty, the stomach makes ghrelin, the hormone that tells the brain to feel hungry. The stomach stops making it when food starts entering it.

● Gastrin also tells the small intestine to start its work (new food is coming) and the large intestine to throw out the old, digested meal.

◀ *The stomach does more than just digest food. It guides the body to eat healthy*

In Real Life

Somatostatin is also known as the growth hormone-inhibiting hormone. It regulates the endocrine system and is secreted by the D cells of the islets to obstruct the release of glucagon and insulin. It also prevents the release of the growth hormone when it is generated in the hypothalamus. So, there have been many studies conducted on the use of the somatostatin hormone on diseases like breast cancer and malignant lymphoma.

The Things that Make Us

30 per cent of our body is made up of proteins, carbohydrates, fats, vitamins and minerals. The remaining 70 per cent is water. Those are exactly the things we need to eat and drink.

▼ *Food items are grouped into different food groups*

 Proteins

This is what you need for building up muscle, repairing tissue and growing up. You get a lot of it from meat, fish, eggs, cheese, beans and lentils. Proteins are made of 20 kinds of amino acids. Our digestive system breaks up proteins into their amino acids and absorbs these. In the body, amino acids do a lot of things, including making the proteins that the body needs. You need to eat proteins every day as the body cannot store them.

 Carbohydrates

You get them in milk, fruits, vegetables and grains like rice, corn, wheat and oats. Our body needs them the most, because these are turned into our daily energy. Carbs are stored in the liver as glycogen, or turned into fats that can be stored in adipose tissue.

Fats

These are our body's energy source in an emergency, as they give more energy by weight compared to carbs. You also need them for absorbing some vitamins, for your nerves to work correctly and to make some important hormones. You get fat from butter, cooking oil, meat and eggs. Fats are stored in adipose tissue, which is found in many tissues and organs in our body.

◀ *Though people say we should drink eight glasses of water every day, this is not a fixed number. You should drink water whenever you feel thirsty*

Proteins

Carbohydrates

Fats

Vitamins

You need very little of these nutrients, but they are vital to our body's health. There are 13 of them and each does a different job:

Vitamin A (found in carrots) is needed for your eyes.

Vitamin B1 (found in fish, eggs and cabbage) helps your body burn sugar. The B-vitamins usually come together in most foods.

Vitamin B2 is needed to make healthy red blood cells (RBCs).

Vitamin B3 controls the amount of fat in the blood.

Vitamin B5 helps in general metabolism, along with **B7**.

Vitamin B6 is needed for making antibodies, haemoglobin and for your nerves to work well.

Vitamin B9 (found in peas and beans) is needed for repairing tissues and making new cells.

Vitamin B12 is needed for making healthy RBCs and keeping the nervous system healthy.

Vitamin C (found in citrus fruits) is needed for skin and bones.

Vitamin D (found in egg yolk and sea fish) helps your body absorb calcium and keep the immune system healthy.

Vitamin E (found in vegetable oils and nuts) helps your immune system.

Vitamin K (found in green vegetables and berries) keeps your bones strong and helps your blood clot properly.

Vitamin supplements

Vitamins and minerals

Minerals

Minerals keep your body healthy in many ways. While you need some minerals in abundance, such as calcium (for making bones), phosphorus (for getting energy), magnesium (blood sugar levels), sodium and potassium (making nerves work), chloride (for acid in the stomach for digestion) and sulphur (for healthy hair), there are other minerals like zinc (for immunity), iron (for haemoglobin), fluoride (for strong teeth), selenium (for healthy cells), manganese (for bone health), copper (for iron absorption), iodine (for making thyroid hormone) and cobalt (for making Vitamin B12), all of which are needed only in little amounts. A healthy diet should give you enough minerals without needing food supplements.

Incredible Individuals

Elsie Widdowson (1906–2000) was a British nutrition scientist who worked out the chemical make-up of many foods. During the Second World War, Britain faced a huge shortage of food. Soon, the British government found out that a simple diet of bread, potatoes and cabbage could provide sufficient nutrition.

The Intestine

Though it is called the 'small' intestine, it is more than three metres long. It is taller than the tallest human that ever existed! To fit all this length, the small intestine coils and loops around itself, like a long rope would tangle around itself. The small intestine does the hard work of digesting all of your food.

Did you know that it also acts like a second tongue? It has the enterochromaffin cells which can sense chemicals that may be harmful to you. These cells send a message to the brain, which acts quickly to make you feel 'sick'. You stop eating and throw out what you have eaten.

▶ *The illustration shows the different internal organs of the digestive system. Notice the large and small intestines in detail*

👤✓ In Real Life

Compared to chimps, our intestines are much shorter. Some scientists suggest that since we have been consuming cooked food for a very long time, our body has evolved to make shorter intestines. This is because cooking helps break down some food, making our body spend less energy on its digestion.

▲ *Human beings need less energy to digest food than chimps since we cook our food*

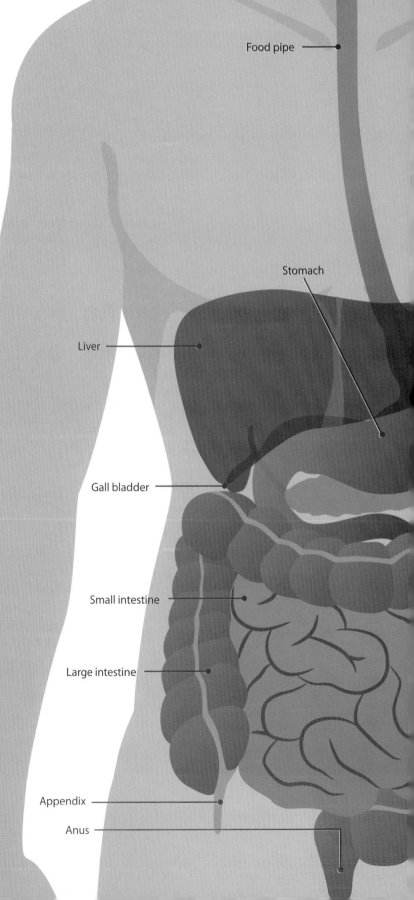

Food pipe

Stomach

Liver

Gall bladder

Small intestine

Large intestine

Appendix

Anus

The Starter Course: Duodenum

The duodenum is the part that receives the partly digested food from the stomach. Two things happen here:

* Bile from the bile duct acts like soap and makes sure that the fat in your food mixes thoroughly with the rest.

* The pancreas pours a big mix of enzymes that digest the rest of the food. They keep working till the food reaches the end of the small intestine.

The Main Course: Jejunum and Ileum

The jejunum starts digestion, and the ileum finishes it. The inner walls of both are made of thousands of tiny fingers called villi. Each of these villi are made of even tinier fingers called microvilli. They make the inside border of the intestine very large, so that enzymes can attack every part of the food. The walls of the intestine contract and expand all the time (peristalsis) to keep pushing the food ahead. They also make some more enzymes.

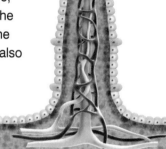

◀ The intestinal wall is made up of thousands of villi and microvilli

▶ A microvillus with arteries and veins ready to absorb digested amino acids and sugars

More Than Just a Digester

The intestine is busy with digestion all day long, but it does other things too. It has tied up with the immune system to create a protective tissue around it called MALT, which keeps bacteria from the intestine escaping into the blood. It also makes a lot of hormones that control digestion, just as the stomach does. One of these hormones is incretin, which tells the pancreas to make another hormone called insulin. Insulin tells the rest of the body to take up the sugar that the intestine just put into the blood.

Another hormone it makes is **serotonin**, which goes to the brain and spinal cord. It tells the nervous system to start the 'rest and digest' system. Serotonin makes the body feel sleepy and convinces the brain that the stomach is full.

Pancreas

⊛ Incredible Individuals

Travellers to Latin America often come down with a kind of diarrhoea called Montezuma's Revenge. This happens because of unhygienic hotel rooms or eating street food, where harmful bacteria irritate the intestine. It is named after Montezuma, the last king of the Aztecs who was killed by the Spanish conquerors.

▶ Montezuma was the last king of the Aztecs. His name is given to a kind of diarrhoea which affects travellers

The Liver

Did you know that the liver is the body's largest gland, weighing nearly 1.4 kg? It has to be, for it is the body's doctor. It is made of cells called hepatocytes. These cells make bile and also deal with a lot of chemicals that may enter the body—toxins in your food, the medicines you take for illness and the wastes made by your tissues. The liver turns them into harmless chemicals that are gotten rid of through urine or bile.

A special vein—the hepatic portal vein—brings blood from the small intestine directly to the liver, where it can remove toxins that came from food and also take up glucose.

▲ Location of the liver in the body

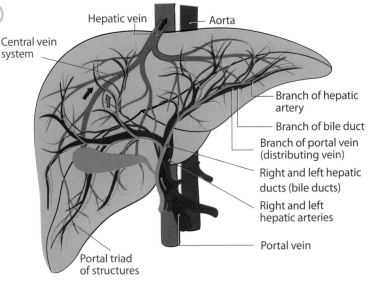

Cholesterol synthesis
Helps in the absorption of vitamins
Glucose   Glycogen
Deactivation of poisons and toxins
Hormones & enzymes production and detoxification
Produces bile
Amino acid synthesis

▲ The liver does many things to keep our body healthy

Storing Glucose

Once you have eaten, your blood suddenly has a lot of sugar in it. Most of this sugar goes to your cells where it is turned into energy. But there is still quite a lot left over. All this goes to the liver, where it turns them into long, stringy molecules called glycogen. If you miss a meal, your brain's hunger centre tells the liver to turn some of the glycogen back into sugar.

Gall Bladder

The liver makes bile all day long, but it cannot store it. Instead, the bile is stored in the gall bladder, where it remains till the brain tells it that food has entered the stomach. Then it pours all the bile into the duodenum, and digestion can begin.

Hepatic vein
Central vein system
Aorta
Branch of hepatic artery
Branch of bile duct
Branch of portal vein (distributing vein)
Right and left hepatic ducts (bile ducts)
Right and left hepatic arteries
Portal vein
Portal triad of structures

▲ The liver is full of veins that help it take up sugar from the blood very quickly

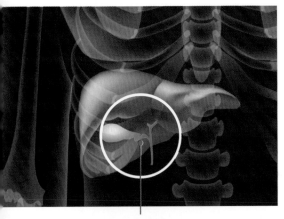
Gall bladder
▲ The gall bladder stores bile until needed. Bile helps in digesting fats

Incredible Individuals

The Ancient Greeks had a myth that the god Prometheus stole fire from the other gods and gave it to humans, who could use it to cook food and stay warm. For this, Prometheus was punished: he was chained to a rock and every day an eagle would peck out his liver. The liver would grow back in the night, and the eagle would come the next day.

▶ A painting showing an eagle pecking out Prometheus' liver. The liver has the astonishing ability of repairing itself

The Pancreas

The pancreas is not one organ but two. Part of it works for the digestive system by making enzymes, while the rest of it makes hormones that help the body stay healthy and active.

The food coming from the stomach is full of acid, which stops the intestine's enzymes from working. Therefore, the pancreas makes a lot of sodium bicarbonate. This reacts with the stomach's acid to make salt, which is then absorbed into the blood. The carbonate is finally removed by your lungs as carbon dioxide.

$$HCl + NaHCO_3 \rightarrow NaCl + H_2CO_3$$

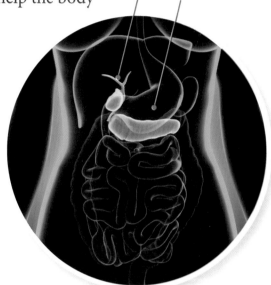

Gall bladder

Pancreas

▲ *Pancreas and gall bladder*

Enzyme-making

The cells of the pancreas that make enzymes are called acinar cells. They make many different kinds of enzymes that can digest proteins, DNA, fats and carbohydrates. The enzymes are collected in tiny pipes that finally flow into the main pancreatic duct.

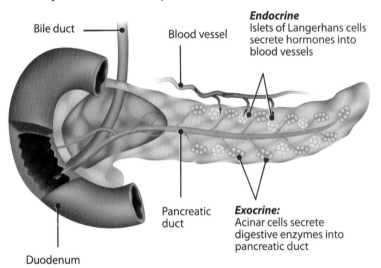

Bile duct

Blood vessel

Endocrine
Islets of Langerhans cells secrete hormones into blood vessels

Pancreatic duct

Exocrine:
Acinar cells secrete digestive enzymes into pancreatic duct

Duodenum

▲ *The pancreas makes both enzymes and hormones. Enzymes are poured into the duodenum, while hormones go into the blood*

💡 Isn't It Amazing!

Diabetes is a disease we get if the body cannot make enough insulin or makes it wrong. Diabetic patients have to take regular injections to live normally. But did you know that most of the insulin they take, comes not from other human beings, but from specially modified bacteria?

▶ *Artificial insulin made by genetically engineered bacteria*

⭐ Incredible Individuals

Insulin has got more people Nobel Prizes than any other molecule.

* In 1923, F G Banting and J. J. R Macleod got it for discovering insulin.
* In 1958, Frederick Sanger got it for finding out its molecular structure.
* In 1977, Rosalyn Yalow got it for finding a method to measure insulin in the body.

▶ *Rosalyn Yalow, who won the 1977 Nobel Prize in Medicine*

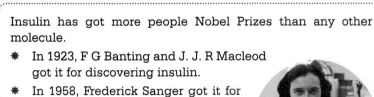 Hormone-making

Hormones are made by a different kind of cell, the Islets of Langerhans. The pancreas makes two important hormones:

* Glucagon, which tells the liver to turn glycogen to glucose. Glucagon is released when your blood has run out of sugar.

* Insulin, which tells your body's cells to take up sugar from the blood. Insulin is released after you have eaten food.

Enzymes: How We Digest Food

We have talked a lot about enzymes, but what exactly are they?
How do they digest food?

Our body makes several thousand different kinds of proteins that do many things. One kind are enzymes—proteins that help carry out biochemical reactions in the body. They do this by acting like tiny locks—each lock can only be opened by a matching key. In the intestine, these keys (called substrate) are the food we eat, like proteins, complex fats and carbs. Each enzyme catches its own substrate and turns it into the product of digestion—amino acids, simple fats and sugars.

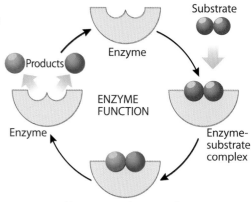

Substrate

Enzyme

Products

ENZYME
FUNCTION

Enzyme

Enzyme-
substrate
complex

Enzyme-product complex

▲ Each enzyme in the digestive system reacts with its own substrate, and nothing else

Enzymes in the Mouth

Amylase is the first enzyme your food meets—in your drool (saliva). It turns starch into sugar. If you hold a thin slice of potato in your mouth for long enough, you can feel it turning sweet. Another enzyme is the lingual lipase, which starts digesting the fat in your food. Your saliva also has lysozyme, an enzyme that breaks up the walls of bacterial cells.

Stomach Enzymes

Pepsin is the main one in the stomach. It breaks proteins into smaller bits called peptides. The stomach also makes gastric lipase, which digests fats. Young children have another called rennin, which helps to digest the protein casein, found in milk and cheese.

◀ After eating, the brain indicates that we rest, so digestion can happen properly

 Bile

To help you digest the fats you eat, the hepatocytes of the liver make bile. Bile is a yellowish-green soap-like liquid, made of bile salts and bile pigments. Bile salts have two parts—a fatty part that ties up fats in your food and a salt part that mixes them with the intestinal juice. Without bile, the fat would stick to the walls of the intestine and slow down digestion.

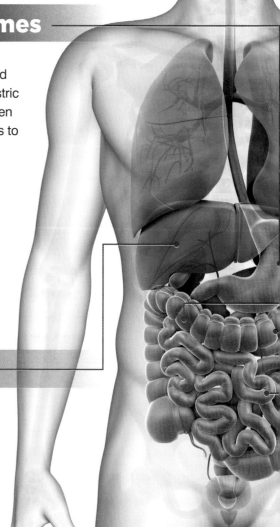

Pancreatic Juice

The pancreas makes a lot of enzymes, which it releases together into the duodenum as pancreatic juice. Here is what they do:

Enzyme	Acts on	End Product
Carboxy-peptidase	Peptides	Amino acids and peptides
Chymotrypsin	Proteins	Peptides
Elastase	Proteins	Peptides
Ribonuclease	RNA	Nucleotides
Deoxyribonuclease	DNA	Nucleotides
Pancreatic amylase	Starch	Sugars
Pancreatic lipase	Complex fats	Simple fats
Trypsin	Proteins	Peptides

 # Enzymes from the Small Intestine

The small intestine's microvilli make the last few enzymes, which finish up digestion.

Enzyme	Acts on	End Product
α-Dextranase	Starch	Glucose
Lactase	Lactose	Glucose and galactose
Maltase	Maltose	Glucose
Sucrase	Sucrose (the most common sugar)	Glucose and fructose
Peptidases	Peptides	Amino acids
Enteropeptidase	Trypsinogen	Trypsin*
Pancreatic lipase	Complex fats	Simple fats
Trypsin	Proteins	Peptides

*The pancreas do not make trypsin directly, because it is a very powerful enzyme which can attack the intestine. So, it is made as trypsinogen, which another enzyme called enteropeptidase turns into trypsin.

 # Lactose Intolerance

Lactose is the sugar present in milk, which is digested by lactase in the small intestine. Some people's bodies stop making lactase as they grow out of childhood. If they consume milk then, they cannot digest the lactose in it. Instead it goes into the large intestine, where bacteria turn it into gas. This is called lactose intolerance.

 # Incredible Individuals

Does the word pepsin sound familiar? In 1893, **Caleb Bradham** introduced a new soda to market as an aid to digestion. '*Pepsia*' is Greek for digestion and cola comes from the name for kola-nut, which is used to make the drink.

Large Intestine and Appendix

Any picture of the digestive system will show it as a big tube curving around the abdomen. However, most of the food has been digested and absorbed in the small intestine. The stomach and the small intestine also make the hormones that tell the brain to get you to rest while you digest. So, what is left for the large intestine to do? Surprisingly, a lot!

Digesting Water

Did you know that every glass of water you drink, must travel the complete length of your digestive system, before it is absorbed? Why wait so long? That is because your digestive system needs all the water to keep the insides of the stomach and intestines moist till the enzymes have done their work.

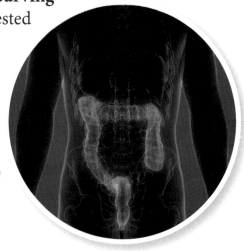

▲ *The large intestine*

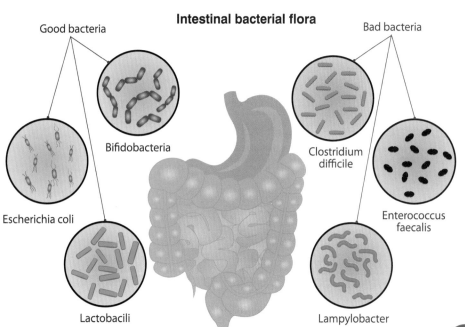

Intestinal bacterial flora

Good bacteria

Bifidobacteria

Escherichia coli

Lactobacili

Bad bacteria

Clostridium difficile

Enterococcus faecalis

Lampylobacter

▲ *Good bacteria make vitamins and keep bad bacteria away*

Bacteria

Most of the digestive system is too dangerous for bacteria to live in. But did you know that trillions of them live in the large intestine, belonging to over 700 species? If you remove them, you would lose valuable friends who make some amino acids as well as Vitamins B7, B9 and K; who help you absorb minerals and break down some carbs. They also keep bad bacteria away.

The Mysterious Appendix

This is a tiny part of the large intestine, near where the small intestine meets it. In 2007, some scientists found out that it may act as a training centre for the immune system, and as a refuge for the bacteria that live in the intestine.

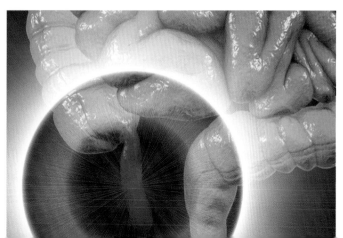

◀ *The painful swelling of the appendix is called appendicitis*

Isn't It Amazing!

A horse's appendix (called caecum) is nearly 4 feet long! In fact, this is true of all plant-eating animals, like cows, goats and rabbits. The caecum is full of bacteria that help digest the complex carbs found in leaves and grasses.

▶ *Plant-eating animals like horses and cows have very large appendices*

Excretion: Eliminating Waste

Once the food has been consumed and all the protein, sugar, fat, vitamins, minerals and water from it has been absorbed for the body's use, the remainder is completely unwanted, and must be eliminated. This is carried out through the process of excretion.

Regular exercise coupled with a timely eating and rest regimen helps in excreting wastes at regular intervals.

Keeping Toxins Out

This is actually the body's way of keeping itself safe from infectious bacteria, viruses and fungi, or from some poisonous things in our food. The small intestine has cells that sniff out toxins. If they find any, the small and large intestinal walls contract very quickly, pushing the food to the anus. It is thrown out, undigested and watery. Diarrhoea is a common symptom experienced by those suffering from cholera and dysentery.

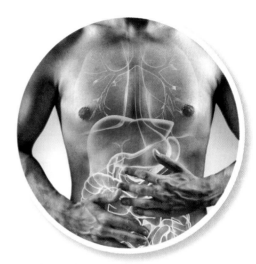

▲ *Diarrhoea causes pain, as the intestines try to shove out food that has gone bad or has bad bacteria in it*

▲ *Grains and greens are rich in fibre, which prevents constipation*

Constipation

This happens if you have not had enough water. By the time food arrives in the large intestine, it becomes very dry, making it hard for the organ to move it along. It also happens if you do not have enough fibre in your diet. Fibre stimulates the intestines to keep shoving food forward. Add 5 to your age, that is the amount of fibre (in grams) that you need every day.

Flatulence

If you have had lots of beans, you hope you do not get this in the classroom. Flatulence happens when the digestive system fills up with gas and has to throw it out, often making a whistling sound. Beans and fibre-rich foods have carbs that cannot be digested by the small intestine. But the bacteria in the large intestine can digest them, producing carbon dioxide. If your bacteria are not healthy, they might produce bad smelling gases.

▶ *Flatulence happens when your large intestine's bacteria break up some food that your small intestine cannot*

Taking Food to Those Who Need It

Once the digestive system has broken down all the food, it needs to get it to the rest of the body, which needs energy and raw materials for growth. But why do we need to digest food in the stomach and intestines before it goes into our bodies? That is because it has to be broken into chemicals like glucose and amino acids that are simple enough to be taken into the blood. This also makes sure that the body has control over what gets into it and what is excreted out.

Active Transport

Different nutrients are taken up by the body in different ways. Tiny little proteins in the walls of the intestine act like pumps to push sugars, minerals and some vitamins into the blood. As the body needs energy to do this, it is called **active transport**.

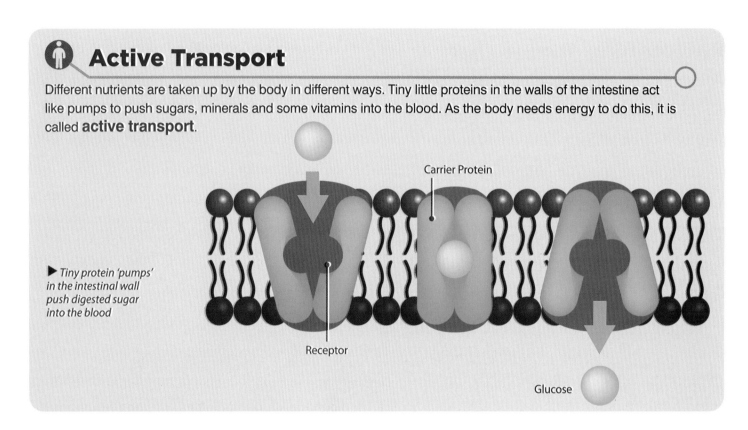

Carrier Protein

Receptor

Glucose

▶ Tiny protein 'pumps' in the intestinal wall push digested sugar into the blood

Isn't It Amazing!

You know that pythons go hungry for many days and then suddenly catch one big meal. But did you know that digesting the meal can take up as much as 37 per cent of the energy the food gives? This makes the python go to a safe place and rest for a few days to digest all of its food.

▲ A python resting after eating a gazelle

Diffusion

This is how many fats and some vitamins are taken up. They pass through the intestine into the blood without any effort. That is why fatty foods seem to be digested faster than sugary foods.

Lipoprotein

Not all fats are allowed to go into the blood directly, as they can clog up your arteries causing plaque. Instead, they are tied with proteins to make **lipoproteins**, which act as escorts in the blood. If a plaque becomes too big, it can block the artery. The organ that gets blood from the artery begins to starve.

▶ Fats stick to the walls of arteries, causing plaque

Metabolism: Make It or Break It

What our cells do with the sugar, fats and amino acids that they take in from blood is called metabolism. When they make things, it is called anabolism. For example, the amino acids are used to make proteins like haemoglobin, insulin or collagen. The fats are used to make the membranes of cells. When they turn them into energy, it is called catabolism. One form of catabolism is cellular respiration.

Cellular Respiration

This is the way the body gets energy from glucose. Blood brings both glucose (from the intestine) and oxygen (from the lungs) to each of the body's cells. They make the oxygen react with the glucose to form carbon dioxide and water.

$$C_6H_{12}O_6 + 6O_2 \rightarrow 6CO_2 + 6H_2O + energy$$

While doing this, a lot of energy is released. This energy (measured in calories) can be used to:

* Make muscles work, so that you can move your arms and legs.

* Make energy to digest food.

* Grow new cells and tissues.

* Strengthen the immune system.

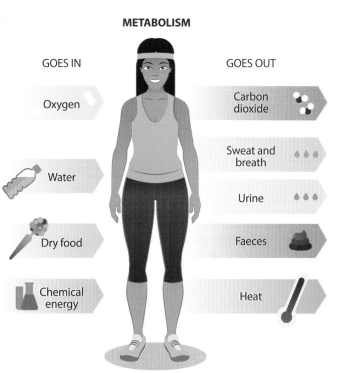

METABOLISM

GOES IN
- Oxygen
- Water
- Dry food
- Chemical energy

GOES OUT
- Carbon dioxide
- Sweat and breath
- Urine
- Faeces
- Heat

▲ *A diagram showing what happens when you go running*

In Real Life

During exercise or heavy work, our muscles use up a lot of energy. As blood cannot supply oxygen fast enough, the muscles use **anaerobic respiration** instead of cellular respiration. During this, the muscles release a lot of lactic acid into blood. Lactic acid builds up and causes pain. If you have overworked, the lactic acid may build up very fast to give you sudden pains called **cramps**.

▲ *A lot of hard work or exercise releases lactic acid, which causes sudden pain in the muscles*

Burning Calories

Did you wonder why some people stay thin even though they eat a lot and some put on weight even though they eat little? That depends on the **basal metabolic rate**, the speed with which the body turns food to energy. If it uses up food very fast, the body is warmer and you feel more energetic. BMR differs from person to person and depends on your genes, diet and overall health.

▲ *Various exercises, including running, help us lose weight*

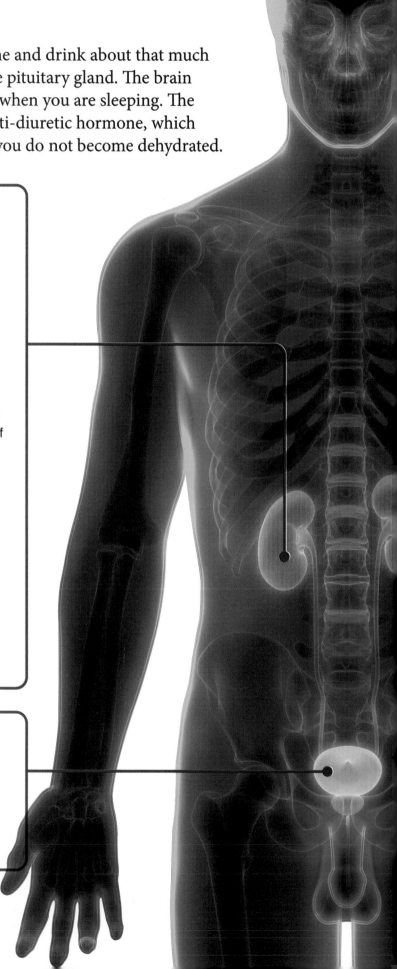

The Urinary System

After your tissues have converted food into metabolites and energy, the remainder is waste. It is drained out by your blood and taken to the urinary system, which filters it and removes it.

In a day, most people will pass 2,500 ml of urine and drink about that much of water. This is controlled by the brain and the pituitary gland. The brain makes sure that you do not need to pass urine when you are sleeping. The pituitary gland makes a hormone called the anti-diuretic hormone, which controls how much water you urinate, so that you do not become dehydrated.

 ## Kidneys

These are two bean-shaped organs near your intestines, which filter the blood. Each kidney is made up of thousands of tiny parts called **nephrons**. Each nephron is made of a tangle of blood capillaries (called glomerulus), which allow the plasma to seep out and enter the cup-shaped Bowman's capsule. The waste travels further through a long tube, shaped like a hairpin (the loop of Henle), where most of the water is reabsorbed by the blood. What remains finally is a thick soup of urea, other wastes and a little water, which becomes urine. The urinary ducts merge at the centre of the kidney to become the **ureters**, which take urine to the bladder.

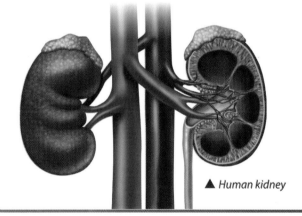

▲ *Human kidney*

 ## Urinary Bladder

Did you know that the urinary bladder can hold up to half a litre of water? It collects the urine from the kidneys till enough has built up. Then the nerves of the bladder tell the brain that it is time to pass urine. The urine finally passes through the urethra out into the environment.

💡 Isn't It Amazing!

Why do male dogs urinate so many times, unlike human beings who have to go all at once? That is because dogs use their urine to mark territory, by widdling on trees, car tyres or streetlights. This is your dog's way of telling other dogs that he's the boss in this area. They can do this because they can control their bladders and let out only small amounts of urine each time.

▶ *A male poodle marks a tree to say that this is his area*

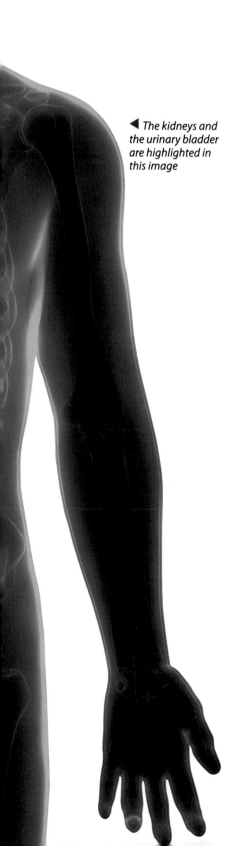

◀ *The kidneys and the urinary bladder are highlighted in this image*

▲ *The colour of your urine says how healthy you are. Usually, a healthy person has clear urine.*

🧍 Healthy and Unhealthy Urine

Did you know that the colour and smell of your urine can tell you how healthy you are? If you are healthy, have been eating regularly and drinking enough water, your urine should be clear, colourless or pale yellow and there should be a lot of it. If you have thick urine which is dark yellow and smelly or cloudy, it means you are ill. If it is red, then your kidneys have been infected, because the red colour shows that blood cells have come into urine.

🧍 Urine Testing

Doctors use a urine test to find out if you are ill. If there are germs in your blood, they may break through your kidneys and show up in urine. If you have jaundice, your urine will have bile. Too much stress may show up as creatine, a yellow-coloured substance. Incorrect metabolism may show many other biochemicals in urine.

👥 In Real Life

Urine is full of urea, which turns into ammonia over time. Stale urine is used to soak animal hides during the making of leather. The ammonia reacts with the hide and softens it and weakens the hair in it. In the past, urine was used as a source of ammonia for washing clothes and making gunpowder.

Tummy Troubles

Our digestive system sometimes goes wrong, giving us an upset stomach. It may be caused by disease, but often it is because we are not eating right. Good habits help keep tummy troubles away. Do not miss breakfast, eat slowly and chew your food well. Ensure you are having fibre, which helps the intestines move the food along. Do not eat at odd hours, like when watching TV, or in the middle of the night, when your body is still digesting dinner. Do not eat when you are stressed, like when studying for an exam. Take a break instead.

▲ *A little boy with indigestion. Healthy eating habits keep it away*

 ## Indigestion

Indigestion is also called **dyspepsia**. You know you have got it when you:

* have pain in the tummy (abdomen)
* feel like vomiting
* keep belching or giving off wind
* have diarrhoea or constipation
* do not feel hungry
* feel that your chest is burning **(heartburn)**

It usually happens because you are under stress (haven't studied for a test?), are not eating properly or on time (too many crisps?), or are sensitive to some foods (like nuts). Adults may get it because they smoke too much, or drink too much coffee or alcohol.

 ## Ulcers

Ulcers are serious ailments that happen when your stomach or duodenum's lining is eroded by the acid in it. These ulcers are not just painful but can also cause severe allergies. Ulcers happen because of stress, and also because of infection by a bacterium called **Helicobacter pylori**.

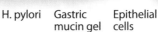

H. pylori Gastric mucin gel Epithelial cells   H. pylori raises pH, mucin de-gels

▲ *The diagram shows how Helicobacter pylori reaches the stomach*

 ## Allergies

Some diseases of the digestive system may happen because of allergies. Coeliac disease, which damages the intestines, is one such kind. You get it if your body is allergic to gluten, a protein found in wheat. Others happen because of infections (like *Helicobacter pylori*), malnourishment, poor eating habits or psychological conditions.

⊙ Incredible Individuals

Barry Marshall was an Australian scientist who was trying to show that Helicobacter pylori caused ulcers, but no one believed him because they thought nothing could live in the acidic environment of the stomach. Then one day, Barry Marshall drank a tube full of this bacterium. Within a week, he began showing the symptoms of ulcers, and could show that he was really infected. He got the Nobel Prize in Medicine in 2005.

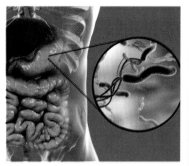

▲ *Helicobacter pylori is a spiral-shaped bacterium that causes stomach and duodenal ulcers*

👤 Irritable Bowel Syndrome

Do you feel crampy and moody most of the time? You may have **irritable bowel syndrome**, which causes diarrhoea in some people and constipation in others, and sometimes both. This is because something affects your large intestine, but we don't know what yet. Eating regularly, eating fibre and keeping bad bacteria out keeps you healthy.

👤 Beriberi and Scurvy

Not having enough vitamins can causes diseases. For example, not having enough Vitamin B1 causes **beriberi**, a disease in which you feel numb and weak, all the time. Not having enough Vitamin C in the body causes bleeding gums, slow wound healing and tiredness. This disease is called **scurvy**.

💡 Isn't It Amazing!

In the early 19th century, sailors in the British Navy were called limeys. This was because they were all forced to drink lemon juice, which contains lots of Vitamin C and prevents scurvy.

👤 Eating Disorders

Some disorders cause people to eat too little or too much food. In anorexia nervosa, people eat too little because they feel they are fat all the time and become severely malnourished. Another disease is **binge-eating disorder**, where the brain's hunger centre does not work correctly, making people feel hungry all the time.

◀ *The illustration shows a person suffering from anorexia nervosa*

👤 Kwashiorkor

Babies who do not get enough protein in their diet get **kwashiorkor**. In many countries, foods rich in protein, like meat, eggs and milk are too expensive, and people instead eat food rich in carbs, like grains and yams. It causes swollen bellies, thin limbs and frequent diarrhoea.

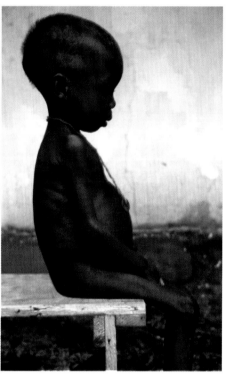

▲ *Kwashiorkor is a disease brought on due to a severe dietary protein deficiency, and this child, whose diet fit such a deficiency profile, presented with symptoms including edema of legs and feet, light-coloured, thinning hair, anaemia, a pot-belly, and shiny skin*

👤 In Real Life

In many diseases or in cases of starvation, your body loses water and minerals very quickly. To replace them, the World Health Organisation (WHO) recommends an **oral rehydration solution**, which has sodium citrate, potassium chloride and glucose. It was tested in refugee camps during the 1971 Bangladesh War by Indian doctor Dilip Mahalanabis. It is now used around the world.

A Healthy Mind & Healthy Body

A diet that has the right amounts of proteins, carbs, fats, vitamins, minerals and water is a balanced diet. However, because of poverty, stress, bad eating habits, or even mental conditions, you may fall short of one or more of these nutrients. This is called **malnutrition**.

If a pregnant woman is malnourished, her baby can be born with many birth defects, including low intelligence, poor immunity and other defects like blindness or deafness. This is particularly true of micronutrients like vitamins and minerals. Malnutrition as a young child may also leave you unable to score well in school.

◀ One must always try to have a hearty and balanced breakfast

▶ Eating a light snack in the evening prevents us from feeling hungry before dinner

Breakfast is Essential... Even If You're in a Hurry

Late for school and not interested in breakfast cereal? But you shouldn't skip it, because breakfast is the most important meal. When you wake up, your body has digested its dinner and both your brain and muscles need fresh energy. A good breakfast does that—it gives you the energy to stay awake and alert in class, and the energy to play in the break.

Snacks are Good for You

Children eat less in meals and like having a snack now and then. Tell mum and dad that that's right for you. It keeps your energy levels up. Fries, crisps and chocolate are high in sugar—have a little if you've not had a meal in a long time. But the best are fruits, muffins, bread-and-butter or nuts.

In Real Life

Athletes go bananas for bananas! That's because bananas are packed with sugar and vitamins and give an instant dose of healthy energy. They are also rich in fibre and stop constipation. Go ahead, have a banana, and then another.

Eat Less, but Eat More

Puzzled? We mean to say, eat less in each meal, but have more meals. Research says that fewer meals make you overeat, while more meals help you eat smaller, healthier portions. A 3-ounce bag of chips actually has 3 servings, so don't eat it all at once. Share it with friends or eat it over 3 days.

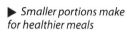

▶ *Smaller portions make for healthier meals*

Sugar and Sleepiness

After eating foods rich in proteins and carbohydrates, like meat and rice, we feel sleepy. This is because the sugar and amino acids entering the blood make the pancreas make more insulin. Insulin pushes sugars and amino acids into the tissues, except for one amino acid called tryptophan. This instead goes into the brain, where it is turned into serotonin. Serotonin tells the brain to slow down and make the body go to sleep. Sleep is good for digestion as it needs energy. If you don't get good sleep, you can have problems digesting food.

◀ *A quick afternoon nap helps digest your lunch*

Coffee is Good... in Small Amounts

Some adults love drinking coffee, sometimes up to 10 cups a day. The caffeine in it keeps them awake and refreshed. It helps them pass urine and maintain water balance. But it is good only as long as they drink under 400 mg of caffeine (which is about four cups of coffee) in a day. Too much caffeine causes more acid to be released in the stomach and stops your body from absorbing calcium. So if mum or dad have a lot of coffee, tell them to go easy!

▶ *The rule for coffee—do not drink more than four cups in a day*

⊙ Incredible Individuals

Gerty Cori (1896–1957) got the Nobel Prize in 1947, with her husband, for finding out what happens when muscles work very hard. They make lactic acid, which goes to the liver to be made into glucose again. During this time you feel tired and need to rest. Gerty Cori did most of her work when men were still opposed to women doing scientific research, but she did not get discouraged and kept working.

Gall & Kidney Stones

Diseases like liver cancer, infections or anaemia cause the gall bladder to form gallstones. Similar things happen in the kidney too, where **kidney stones** are formed. Doctors know you have got them if:

* you feel a lot of pain in your belly or your back;
* there is blood when you urinate or excrete;
* you get fever and shivering;
* your urine looks cloudy or your excreta looks pale;
* your urethra burns when you pass urine.

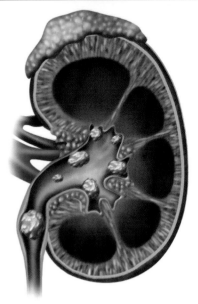

▲ The diagram shows a dissected human kidney

Gallstones

A gallstone is formed when bile becomes very thick due to lack of water, and the bile salts begin to crystallise. These tiny crystals then block the bile duct, causing a lot of pain and indigestion (because bile does not reach the intestine). Gallstones may often have to be removed by surgery.

◀ Gallstones cause lasting, severe pain and indigestion

▶ Kidney stones taken out after surgery. They can grow upto 5 mm wide

Kidney Stones

Drinking a lot of water every day usually stops kidney stones from forming. If there's too little water in the body, the salts and urea filtered from the blood into the kidney begin to crystallise. These stones block the ureters and can cause a lot of pain.

Ultrasound

Certain sounds with an ultrasonic frequency are inaudible to the human ear. Such sounds are known as ultrasound. The vibrations caused by this sound can help break up kidney stones and gall stones in the body into tiny pieces that come out easily and unblock the kidneys or gall bladder. This helps you avoid surgery.

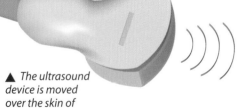

▲ The ultrasound device is moved over the skin of the stomach

⊙ Incredible Individuals

Alexander, the Greek conqueror, died in great pain when he was just 33. Some medical historians believe that the symptoms of his disease described by the writers of his time, point to an inflammation of the gall bladder **(cholecystitis)**, which is usually caused by gallstones.

▶ A mosaic of Alexander of Macedon, from Pompeii. Some historians believe that he died of a gall bladder inflammation

When Organs Give Up

Our kidneys and digestive system are at work throughout our lives, without any rest. Sometimes, because of stress, poor nutrition, disease or old age, they may fail completely. If the artery that supplies blood to the organ is clogged with a plaque, the organ may be starved of nutrients and oxygen, and its cells begin to die.

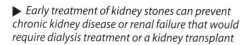

Kidney Failure

When one or both kidneys fail, they are no longer able to filter out toxins from your blood. These toxins then accumulate, causing all kinds of damage to your tissue. Most people with kidney failure have to go to the hospital for **dialysis**, every week. This is a medical procedure by which your blood is filtered by a machine and the clean blood is put back into you.

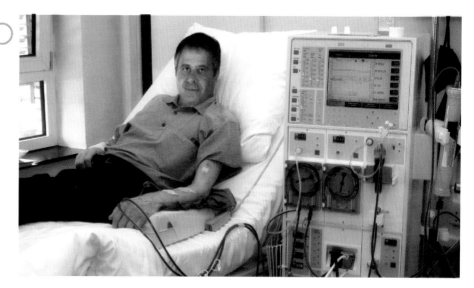

▶ *Early treatment of kidney stones can prevent chronic kidney disease or renal failure that would require dialysis treatment or a kidney transplant*

Organ Transplants

Did you know that you can have your large intestine, appendix or spleen removed without much harm? But some organs, like the liver, heart or kidneys cannot be removed without putting in a new one. This is called an organ transplant.

You need a healthy human **donor** who can give you one of their organs if your kidney or liver fails. But for a donation to work, the donor must match you as closely as possible genetically, such as a parent, sister or brother. Otherwise, your immune system will treat the new organ like it treats germs and destroy it.

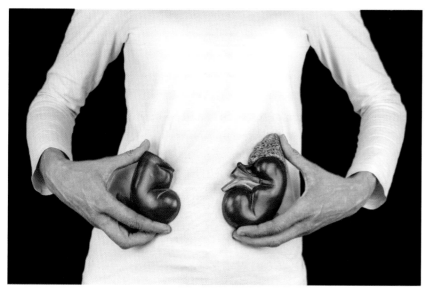

▲ *Kidney replacement requires a perfect match*

In Real Life

Scientists are trying to find out how you can grow your organ again, rather than get it from another person. They do this by studying the **stem cells**, which are cells that grow in all organs, and can turn themselves into any kind of cell. If the right biochemical instructions are given, stem cells can become different tissues and finally make a new organ.

▲ *The photograph shows a close-up of a cell in the human body. Stem cells are studied in the field of cellular therapy and regeneration*

Word Check

Active transport: It is the way by which some food is pumped from your intestines to blood.

Anaerobic respiration: It is the way in which muscles work without enough oxygen, making a lot of lactic acid.

Basal metabolic rate: It is the speed with which your body turns food into energy.

Beriberi: It is a disease caused by not having enough Vitamin B1 in one's diet.

Binge-eating disorder: It is a disorder that makes you overeat because your brain's hunger centre isn't working properly.

Caries: It is the medical name for tooth cavities.

Cavities: It is a disease of the teeth caused by bacteria growing on the sugar on your teeth.

Cholecystitis: It is the inflammation of the gall bladder.

Cramps: It is used to refer to sudden pain in the muscles due to a build-up of lactic acid.

Dialysis: It is the way blood is filtered outside the body.

Digestive system: It is the set of organs and biochemicals that help you eat food, digest it and remove waste.

Donor: It is a person who can give a healthy organ to a person whose organ has failed.

Dyspepsia: It is the medical word for indigestion.

Gag reflex: It is the throat's defence against choking by making you spit out what you've swallowed.

Heartburn: A burning feeling in the chest caused by indigestion.

Helicobacter pylori: It is a bacterium that infects the stomach and causes ulcers.

Hormones: They are the different kinds of biochemicals that act as messengers between organs.

Irritable bowel syndrome: It is a set of conditions that make you uncomfortable, with either diarrhoea, constipation or both.

Kidney stones: They are crystals of urea or salts that form in your kidneys.

Kwashiorkor: It is a disease caused by not having enough protein in one's diet.

Lipoproteins: They are the proteins that help escort fat to tissues through the blood and stop them from sticking to the walls of your arteries.

Malnutrition: It is a disorder caused by not having enough food or certain nutrients in food.

Mandible: It is the lower jaw, which can move.

Maxilla: It is the upper jaw, which cannot move.

Metabolism: It is the way in which your body turns food into energy, or uses it to make tissue parts.

Nephrons: They are the tiny parts of the kidney that filter blood.

Oral rehydration solution: It is a mixture of sodium citrate, potassium chloride and glucose dissolved in water and given to patients suffering from dehydration.

Pharynx: It is the inside of your throat, where the windpipe and food pipe cross each other.

Root canal operation: It is a medical procedure in which dentists remove rotten tissue from inside your teeth.

Scurvy: It is a disease caused by not having enough Vitamin C in food.

Serotonin: It is the chemical in your brain that tells it to make you go to sleep.

Stem cells: They are the cells in the body that can turn themselves into any kind of cell and help repair organs.

Thyroid gland: It is an organ in the throat that makes the thyroid hormone.

Thyroid hormone: It is a hormone that helps the body make energy from food, helping you grow.

Ulcers: They are wounds inside the lining of the digestive system, often caused by Helicobacter pylori.

Ureters: Tubes that take urine from the kidneys to the urinary bladder.